Gratitudes:
To Our Mothers

Austie M. Baird
-Editor, Cover Artist-

Austie M. Baird is a born and raised Oregonian, holding both History and Education degrees from Eastern Oregon University. Long before becoming a wife and mother, Baird connected with the power of the written word, finding healing properties in both reading and writing. She draws strength from the beauty that surrounds her and the overwhelming love of her family.

A.B.Baird Publishing
Oregon, USA

Copyright © 2019 by A.B.Baird Publishing

All rights reserved. This book or any portion thereof may not be reproduced or used in any manner whatsoever without the express written permission of the publisher except for the use of brief quotations in a book review.

Printed in the United States of America

First Printing, 2019

ISBN: 978-1-949321-05-0
Library of Congress Control Number: 2019903487

All writings within this anthology belong to the author to which they are credited. Contributing authors maintain the copyrights for each piece submitted and published within this anthology.

Cover Art Image by Austie M. Baird

A.B.Baird Publishing
66548 Highway 203
La Grande OR, 97850
USA

www.abbairdpublishing.com

Dear Mothers,

We dedicate these words to you. For the times that you stood by our sides, for the times you had our backs, for the times you lead us by the hand — we thank you for your never-ending devotion to our success... especially in those moments that we could not see your struggles through our own. Your soothing words, giving natures, and (perhaps not always so gentle) guidance has shaped us into the people that we are today. We know now that we may not always see eye to eye about the world, or our personal approaches to it, but when all is said and done we are on the same team as we take our journeys.

Please accept these words, gathered from writers from around the world, as simple tokens of gratitude for all that you do to help make us all that we are. We could not do this, we could not be us, without you.

We are forever grateful, forever loving, and forever yours.

Thank you Mom.

Table of Contents

Author Recognition
Essence: Of Our Mothers

Beauty in the Depths	p.4
Promise	p.5
On the Day the Sky Cried	p.5
Mommy's Bed	p.6
My Mothers Commandments	p.6
She Taught Me This	p.7
Selfless	p.8
Small Faith	p.8
Heart of Her	p.9
Umbilical	p.10
Can You Sing Your Song?	p.11
Beyond	p.11
Motherhood	p.12
A Mother's Love	p.13
Lilac Love	p.13
Motherhood	p.14

To: Our Mothers

Creation- An Ode to my Mother	p.16
The Star to Your Galaxy	p.17
Ode to My Mother's Love	p.18
Life Guard	p. 19
A Haiku to My Mother	p.19
Strawberry	p.20
Without You	p.20
You're Everything	p.20
Collecting Calls #1	p.21
Orange Blood Orange	p.22
All That You Are	p.23
My Mom	p.24
My Angel on the Living Earth	p.24
God	p.25
Seasons- An Ode to my Mother	p.26

Growing Pains
- Mom — p.29
- The Artist — p.33
- The Giver — p.34
- A Mother Without Patience — p.34
- Left-Handed — p.36
- An Original Masterpiece — p.39
- Ivy in the Kitchen — p.40
- Airbag Mother — p.43
- Despite — p.44
- Silence — p.44
- Giving Her the Sun — p.46
- Like Mother, Like Daughter — p.48
- My Mom, Her Thoughts — p.48
- A Candid Grace — p.50
- 02.04.19 — p.50

Looking Back
- A Mother's Love — p.52
- Home From Work — p.52
- The Nest — p.54
- Angelic Purity — p.55
- Courage — p.56
- Gifts To You — p.56
- Steps — p.58
- Thank you for the Whispers — p.59
- Balanced — p.59
- Twilight — p.60
- Symbiotic Blessings — p.61

Generations
- Reflections — p.63
- A Mother's Love — p.64
- Our Love Collides — p.65
- Apologies — p.66

Summoning the Shechinah	p.67
If Family is a Meal	p.68

Memories & Wishes

You Will Know	p.74
The Little Things	p.75
Sentinel	p.75
Mommy Dearest	p.76
You See	p.78
Bare Snow	p.80
Together	p.80
Dance	p.81
My Mother Divine	p.81
A: De:	p.82
What I Want (Choose) to Remember	p.83
Returning to You	p.85
Driving My Mother to Acupuncture	p.86
Transcending Love	p.88
In Memory of Marit Josten Highland	p.90
Grateful	p.92

Competition Results	p.93
Index	p.94-95
Letter to our Readers	p.96
Memorial Dedication	p.97

Gratitudes

Authors

Work from the following authors can be found in the pages of this book. These 36 authors represent sons and daughters from around the world. To learn more about each author please visit them on their main writing platforms on Instagram. For a list of which pages to find each of your favorites, please visit the index at the back of the book.

Abi Hayes	@abi_adventures_
Ambica Gossain	@Tryst_with_fiction
Andigrace	@andigrace_me
Andrew C. Ulon	@AndrewCPoetry
Angela Marie Niemiec	@angel_writer
Araz Sharma	@arazsharma
Austie M. Baird	@glass_walls_life
Ben Hand	@infinityblues86
Danielle Langin	@daniellelangin_
Debjeet Mukherjee	@authordebjeet
Dre Jones	@jones_dre_md
Elizabeth Bonaiuto	@myunrequitedwords
Emily Adams-Aucoin	@emilyapoetry
Emily Louise Witthohn	@e.louise.w
Erica Rolston	@whenthesunrose
Gregory Oman	@ greg.oman
Kevin Vargo	@kevinvargo_
Krystal Centinello	
L.T. Pelle	@l.t.pelle
Lacie Wright	@cowgirllaw
Lara Decastecker	@laradraemi
Lesley Worthington	@worthywrites
LiAnnah Jameson	@liannahjameson
Linda Lokhee	@lindalokheeauthor
Lizzy in Words	@lizzyinwords

Authors

M.R.S	@mrs_poems
Mari Antoinette	
Maya Ephick	@m.g.petri
Megan Fulton	
Megan Hann	
RJK	@ironrosewrites
Russell E. Willis	
Sara Kelly	@sarakelly
Sophia Luna	
Tor Strand	@ tor_strand
Yiskah Rosenfeld	

Essence of our Mothers:

Beauty in the Depths

There is a quiet beauty in the depths of her.

Stillness that shines calm,
Like a lake cradled in shores.

She's cradled and nourished
Those that hips never bore.

Stillness flooding chaos,
Her arrival was the spring.

The awakening of the dirt
As earth learned to breathe again.

There is a quiet beauty in the depths of her.

Enough to drown in,
though she's determined all who enter , swim.

Gently suckling
From her easy ebbs and flows.

No crashing of waves disturbed her peace,
As she keep peace for the broken pieces
Growing beauty in shipwreck reefs.

There is a quiet beauty in the depths of her;
My mother,
Woman, whom I adore.

-Austie M. Baird

Promise

A mother's love
is a band-aid
in a wounding world.
It is a single light bulb
in the confusion
of the darkness.
It is a beacon of hope,
and a promise:
"Everything is going
to be okay."

-Sara Kelly

Mother of Storms

on the day the sky cried
my mother took me into her arms
and promised I'd survive even the most
torrential storms
that's the day I learned
my mother's arms
were the strongest pillar of support
and the softest place to fall

-M.R.S

Mommy's Bed

There are no monsters,
Under the covers,
Of Mommy's Bed

-Austie M. Baird

My Mother's Commandments

do not settle for lust disguised as love
remember your roots, for they will ground you
be resilient
be strong
affirm your worth every day
your body is a temple, cherish it
choose happiness
love your partner madly
sing loudly
believe you can

-M.R.S

She Taught Me This

A true warrior wakes every day
fighting battles no one hears about,
and still finds the will to keep going
when all her muscles burn in pain.

With courage, she protects with ferocious strength,
she does more in a day than most do in a week,
making sure everyone else is happy first,
never showing frustration
regardless of the day's length.

Always going the extra mile,
she is selfless for her passion,
just to hand every victory over to her children,
the reward is just to see their smile.

Going even further
when her feet can't take another step,
she will rise to the challenge,
never getting a break,
no vacation, no rest.

Working tirelessly day and night
to provide the very best,
she is the reason why I'm so strong,
she is my mother,
and to her all my love and gratitude belongs.

-Angela Marie Niemiec

Selfless Mother

how she kneels there
arms wide open
head toward the sky
asking the creator
to lift my pain
and strike her instead
is what makes her such
a selfless mother

-M.R.S.

Small Faith

She keeps my small faith in
her jewelry box next
to decades of gifts that are
mostly handmade or
fragile, more for
protecting than for wearing

(I don't think
we knew we were
assigning her
this responsibility).

but she is an expert.
a professional at keeping
delicate things.

& here I am as proof,
eyes wide with gratitude;
faith still safe & growing.

-Emily Adams-Aucoin

The Heart of Her

She's the kind of woman
Everyone wishes they could be:
Gifting love and acceptance
For all that she sees.

Walk in her kitchen
-The heart of her home-
Sample her love,
As she invites you to become
One of her own.

Never hesitating
Always helping
-Making the most of her role-
My mother, their Nanny
The giver of all things happy.

Celebrations were found
-And capitalized upon-
For no reason was too small
To celebrate our love on.

Laughter and love
Echo among her walls;
A home never empty,
As she created it all.

-Austie M. Baird-

Umbilical

A mother is a man's first love.
His introduction to both the emotional spectrum and femininity.
A star sapphire in a past life,
she stands proud and profound in her purple aura of adoration.
Godiva skin that would drive Willy wonka.
Hair like midnight silk,
softly pulled back like satin curtains presenting the stage of her face.
Caramel eyes that could cause one to melt.
Three chocolate chip freckles perfectly dabbed on each cheek.
The coveted nose our family carries through the generations,
Granny's personal paternity test; our nasal passage.
And then the smile.
Her smile, my smile, our smile, THE smile.
An Amazon's lasso of truth.
Many have fallen in the glimmer of her gold tooth;
a pocket dimension of poppies and lilacs where the world can be perfect and reality sleep.
A bannister when life's stairs get too steep.
A smile a man can fall into and weep.
Then laughter ensues and fear falls through the cracks
An ecliptic love which goes unmatched.
Eternally connected,
    sometimes by noose or leash
        others bungee and tether
But that cord still gives man nutrients he needs,
        That bond lasts forever.

-Dre Jones -

Can You Sing Your Song?

each night in my dreams
i'd swear i had died
until your voice came
to save
and sing me back to sleep
as i laid my head down
on my twin-sized sheets.

-Kevin Vargo

Beyond

If there is a piece of me
that is also hers,
it lives somewhere
in the heart-
how it opens so
willingly.
how it swells &
stretches to hold
all of this
love that is
beyond beyond beyond.

-Emily Adams-Aucoin

Motherhood

what it means to be mother:
holy placement in
trembling, outstretched arms-
you find what steadies

through desperate prayer
through painstaking, deliberate
trial & error

you understand sometimes
& slowly

& at some point,
(who can separate
the hours?)
while gazing at the sleeping
being that breathes &
laughs & lives

& looks a lot like an answer to
a question you inherited-

you accept the gift.

-Emily Adams-Aucoin

A Mother's Love

A mother's love is everything,
There is nothing that compares,
A mother's love is life giving,
With every sacrifice she bears,
And when her children grow and fly,
Away to find their newer skies,
A mother's love may well cry,
For a mother's love true never dies!

- Andrew C. Ulon

Lilac Love

A mother's love means planting a hedge of lilacs
-even though you are allergic-
Simply to watch the joy in your daughters heart
As she stops to smell her favorite flower.

-Austie M. Baird

Motherhood

Mostly mayhem and madness
Obsessive worry about unlikely scenarios
Thankless and tiring a lot of the time
Hoping I'm doing a few things right
Entertaining, exhausting, exciting, endearing, emotional, embarrassing, extraordinary
Reading aloud to curious, innocent souls
Hellish days interspersed with heartwarming contentedness
Obstinate toddler tantrums and outrageous teen angst
Overwhelming moments of gratitude and joy
Don't blink

-Lesley Worthington

Gratitudes

:To Our Mothers:

Creation- An Ode to my Mother

You created me
Out of love
So that I myself
Could laugh
And dance
And explore
The vast and beautiful world
So that I myself
Could love
And I will honor your 9- month creation
By following in your footsteps
Imprinted along my path
And do just that

- Megan Fulton

The Star to Your Galaxy

dear mother,

you brought me up from the group and placed me high up in the sky.
you ignited my kindling flames and they now burn bright with power.
you gifted me with a mentality of determination and the love to help.

you gave me hope.
you made me the north star.

you bestowed me strength.
you bestowed me power.
you bestowed me love.

still, I look to you for guidance.
i look to you for guidance because i merely shine in your galaxy. you are the gravity in our family. you have the capacity to keep us all happy with the love you show us you have every day.

Thank you for letting me shine. thank you for sparking the twinkles in my eyes.

Love, your star.

- Lara Decastecker

Gratitudes

Ode to My Mother's Love

Your humor and artistic hand taught me how to handle the world while your love taught me how to love myself before anyone else

From my wit to my hips I am you
Through and through
You are my mother but also my very best friend

Thank you for being my first home,
And for shining the light but never telling me which way to go

- I am me because of you

-Erica Rolston

Keeping Afloat

You wrote poetry about me
as I slept
and kicked beneath white sheets.
You saw a beauty in my movements
and claimed them on paper,
keeping your daughter afloat
as she battled the waves of dreaming.
Even now,
with long limbs,
how could I drown
knowing your hymns and soft skin
would lift me back into comfort?
Still swimming on beside me,
keeping my head above water.

-Maya Elphick

A Haiku To My Mother

my heartbeat came from your chest
your breath filled my lungs
I sing the songs you needed

-Lacie Wright

Gratitudes

Strawberry

Mother,
your dear strawberry heart
with its exposed seeds
    I'll eat it slowly
    I'll eat it slowly
  is that not what it means to be a daughter?
  to know
  how sweet a heart can taste...

- L. T. Pelle

Your Poem

    Poetry can only go so far.
      I love you
  and would be nothing without you.

      -Maya Elphick

You're Everything

Ma, you're the reason I believe the stars are always within my reach.
If you ever thought me wrong, you still pushed me to keep going strong.
You are the match lighting the way when insecurity browbeat my resolve to sway.
You are the heart behind my courage, beating just to see me flourish.
You are the spring in my stride, the keeper of my pride.

-Ambica Gossain

Collecting Calls # 1: Mama's Boy

How can a telephoned 'hello' make me feel so safe?
Your words are still like band-aids to my boo-boos,
the superhero kind that made me invincible despite my scars.
Black Ranger Power Activate!

Your love makes me great.
Like air thrusters sealed on Nike Soles,
your faith makes ascension possible.
Positioning your 'pumpkins' for MVP posters,
Jordan '98

A deep tissue massage to my mental state.
Your 'good nights' sound like Hershey,
a sweet kiss to wrap daily tensions and tuck them in
It helps my dreams to not deviate.

I appreciate you for calling me today.
(And yes ma'am, I promise I ate).

-Dre Jones

Orange Blood Orange

Mother,
even these gratitudes
are pulled like orange slices
from a ripened heart.
2 daughters
fruited from your ruby flesh.
You taught us how to be grateful
(and for that we are so grateful).
You showed us how to love,
to pluck our own
hearts from your grove.

- L. T. Pelle

All That You Are

oh, mother,
you are the sun
in miami.
the rain
in seattle.
the wind
in chicago,
and the snow
in buffalo.

you are the words
to the poem
and the subject
of the poem itself.

and, mother, you are the book
and the plot
and the author
and the editor
to the greatest novel
i have ever known.

purely put,
you are all-encompassing;
your presence, everlasting.
and you are what makes us,
us -
the identity
the heartbeat
the breath
of our life.

-Kevin Vargo

My Mom

Mom
From dusk to dawn
Sunrise to sunset
You always have my back
Mothers heart never runs empty
Always there for me
Like a lion so strong
Mom
Strong, so lion alike
Me, for there always
Empty runs, never heart mother
Back, my always have you
Dawn to dusk from
Mom

-Mari Antoinette

My Angel on the Living Earth

You taught me to walk and talk.
You still do.
You taught me how to feed and clothe myself.
You still do.
You picked me up whenever I fell,
built me up whenever life got heavy,
gave me advice to get me ready.
You still do.
Thank you.
Mum.
I love you.

-Ben Hand

God

It's incredible how you love me with such vociferous
 intensity,
when all I did was dispossess you of your own
 identity,
your body unrecognizable in its untoward shape and
 size
and your emotions a shamble with the hormone
 override.
And if ever the day comes when I am in doubt of God's
 existence,
I need only to look back at my miraculous inception;
to disentangle the compelling answers intricately sewn
 into the sound of your
voice resounding through the amniotic fluid,
in the gush of the blood we shared through the
 umbilical cord,
in the beat of your heart that kept me going strong,
in the warmth of your embrace as I grew in leaps and
 bounds
and lastly through your eyes where the world is
 always beautiful.
There I am home.

- Ambica Gossain

Seasons- An Ode to my Mother

The long quiet nights
Rocking me to sleep
Helping me explore my new-found world
Letting me wonder
With big green eyes
The same shade as the meadows I played in
Wild and free
Giggling and falling
Into the soft grass
Into your welcoming arms
The same shade as yours
When you looked at me
Thankful that the universe brought us together
Those nights turned into hot summer days
Where you would pick me up and swing me
My feet dancing in the cool breeze
Innocent and full of hope
Catching me as I exclaimed with joy
Instilling in me trust
That you would always catch me
Creating snow angels
In the fallen snow
Delicate on our rosy cheeks
As we sipped peppermint hot coco
You learned to make from your mother
And wishing for more snow
So that we could spend more time
Away from the chaos of the world spinning around us
Just me and you

Jumping in the leaves as they came down
Teaching me the importance of change
And new beginnings
Wiping my tears
As my favorite plant withered
Even though I watered it religiously
Promising me it would come back
With the sun
Instilling in me patience
And you were always right
The sun warmed our freckles
And soon enough my little daisy
Sprung back to life
And once again it was
Just us against the world

- Megan Fulton

:Growing Pains:

Mom

An immense amount of pain,
Handing over your body to the devil,
You endured, oh you were slain,
To give birth to a little me,
Smiling through the tears,
Oh how were you so carefree?
While the family with joy celebrated,
You lay on the hospital bed, exhausted.
And since that day, you were always,
Giving your hundred percent,
Not caring for rewards or praise,
You are purer than all Angels,
More precious than all pearls,
Brighter than a thousand suns combined,
With an iron will, for me, you day and night grind,
Put me before anything else,
Clear paths for me,
When the fog is at its most dense,
Sell your blood,
Make pools of tears and sweat glean,
Go through the mud,
To keep me clean,
oh how will I ever repay this debt?

I drank your milk,
Slept in your arms,
You gave me a house of silk,
With a concoction of charms,
I was ignorant of your love divine,
Callous, selfish, and a fool,
But nonetheless you made the stars shine,
With my wishes like silver fishes in a pool.

Gratitudes

Whenever my candle was at the verge of an end,
You blew it a new life fresh,
Giving me a fiery light, beautifully you mend,
When the night seemed dark and cold,
And life like a dementor's icy breath,
A hug of yours could make my iron gold,
Force the Dawn out of the shadows,
to keep away the grave and the wreath.

I was a dreamer, living in a world unreal,
Wanting things surreal, hopelessly lost,
But you were unfazed, you made a deal,
To make them a reality at any cost,
You didn't care,
For your blood given in exchange,
No matter what the fare,
You won my battles on all turfs simple or strange.
And when the dreams,
were beyond my reach,
You told me,
Reality is not as limited as it seems.
You harboured the sinner,
Treating him like the winner,
You did something bizarre,
When the near seemed far,
Mom, you lied,
Telling me I was perfect,
That none was better than her son,
That I deserved all the respect,
That I was brighter than the Sun,
Yes Mom you lied,
I knew it all that time,
Yes I spied,
But the truth is,

I love the way you lie,

For your lies forged me wings to fly,
To make them truth,
Taught me to always give it another try!!!

Not precious to me are the finest of diamonds,
Emeralds, topaz or tons of gold,
The ultimate treasures are our memories old,
And new we create every instant,
When a phone connects from far distant,
To feel your love through the handset,
Yearning for the hands,
which for months haven't met,
But millineas wouldn't be enough,
for me to forget,
The warmth of a mother's hug,
Light of her eyes,
Brighter than all suns combined,
Nowhere else in this universe you can find.
The softness of her skin,
The kindness in her voice,
Can make your worst losses into wins,
Her tears wash away all your sins,
Her voice a balm to your wounds,
Her demeanor calm as a lake,
With her by your side,
Fearless you remain as you put all on stake,
Her touch fades all scars,
Her words are therapeutic,
Her optimism fantastic,
Her kiss the cure to every disease,
And she's your ultimate body guard,
Under her supervision, do as you please!!

Mothers are definition of perfect,
The quintessential Angels,
Embodiment of Love, Humility and Respect,

Gratitudes

Infinite generators of affection,
Not to mention amazing mentors,
Driving us all to perfection,
They are our alarm clocks and P.As,
Our doctors and nutritionists,
Telling us to eat veggies not Lays,
They are the real Superwomen,
Juggling home, work and kids,
Giving their best 24/7,
Miraculously up to every challenge,
Mightier than the Avengers,
Stronger than the Justice League,
They've truly shown,
That they are in a league of their own!!!

So in the end,
I can just thank you,
For no matter how much love I send,
It will never be equal to what I receive from you
Thank you Mom,
For bringing excitement to this world mundane,
Thank you for bearing so much pain,
Thank you for helping my ship sail,
For telling me goodnight stories,
And many a tale,
Thank you for your scrumptious dishes,
For fulfilling all my wishes,
Thank you for changing my diapers,
For chasing me to eat my meals,
For all memories captured on reels,
Thank you for filling in the gaps,
For singing me lullabies for all those naps,

For making me feel on the top of the world,
For it is with your love impearled,
The list goes on and on,

It's an impossible task,
So I must ask,
How many thanks will be enough?
To tell you, Mom dear,
You are the stuff,
That dreams are made of!!!

- Araz Sharma

Tools

You gave me my first chisel
to carve out my independence,
and my first hammer
to build myself
before letting others hand me blueprints.

-Maya Elphick

The Giver

i take
and take
and take
and take
you give
and give
and give
and give
mother, i am so sorry
for helping myself
to seconds
and thirds
and fourths
mother, it's astonishing
how you're never emptied

-M.R.S.

A Mother Without Patience

Leaves crunch under my feet as
I take these first hollow steps,
a bird flutters his fliers in a nearby tree,
and I watch as the branches bounce in reply
to the wind which flutters too.

Fresh clay mud splatters along the trail,
and before long I miss you and
I don't let it slow me down,
I let it speed me up.

A day of hiking, I thought would help
because six weeks without speaking to your
mother seems too long, and soon
my breathing becomes heavy as I climb higher,
and the spring air forms a chill.

Memories of our last conversation
make my heart race and my knuckles clench,
for how could you bring me to this world
and still understand me so little?

Tree trunks move faster and gravel
crumbles along with dirt, I spot
a darling pink bracelet and I'm swept with
instant compassion for a nameless little girl with a naked wrist,
and a mother lacking patience.

Surely she'd meant to pick it up,
she'd meant to kneel down and place the fragile,
rose-colored beads back in their rightful place,
but hiking with children is hard,
and I haven't called her either.

Snow and ice crunch under my feet as
I take these last few — pounding — steps,
a mother bird settles her wings around her tiny companions,
and we the animals find home under the leaves.

-Emily Louise Witthohn

Left-Handed

sequoias are the tallest, strongest, oldest trees in the world, towering hundreds of feet over everything around them. they can withstand almost anything; but they burn all the time.

the way they grow is when flames climb up their trunks and turn everything inside to dusty ashes. they burn. they grow tall and stately while fire burns away everything they don't need.

probably some of what they do need, too.

my mom was paralyzed a week before her first birthday. she still doesn't know if she was dropped or shaken.

she's left-handed. she likes to joke about being in a secret club, as if I don't know that the only reason her left hand is stronger is because her right side was paralyzed before she could speak.

as if I could forget that she's only left-handed because the people who were supposed to protect her from all the hurt in the world were the ones who hurt her the most.

I've never laughed at that joke.

I don't know how sequoias control their fire; how their outsides can be strong enough to stand even while their insides burn. it seems impossible. they crack, they crumble into scorched pieces. while the smaller trees around them go up in flames, sequoias live; they grow.

they burn.

it was my mom's grandma, not her mother, who taught her to sit tall in a chair. grandmummy lived to be a hundred and one. by that time, her outsides and her insides were failing her and she didn't want to be alive anymore.

she got cremated when she died. I think grandmummy preferred to be ashes than papery flesh and brittle bones. ashes can't be burned.

you can't burn something twice.

I once found myself wincing when I heard my mom say "I love you"
 to her mother on the phone. she just sat tall and straight in her chair and smiled at the forest green paint peeling above the stove.

I guess I don't understand forgiveness yet.

"I love you"

I pretend that I don't think about babies falling every time my mom's embrace makes me feel safe, I pretend that a

mother's love is magical and that sequoias are magical
and that the branches of an ancient tree can
catch a screaming child.

"I love you"

I don't know if sequoias love the fire or if the ashes love
the bark or if the ashes love the trees or if the fire loves
the ashes. but I can't imagine that they do.

this poem could be a parallel between trees and my
family, but it's not. not really.

in our family, it's the ashes that are the strongest. while
the rest rots, ashes hold us up

-Sophia Luna

An Original Masterpiece

each stroke, original
not to be repeated
layered composition
never to be deleted
annoyance flares, attitude
different generation
reign impatience
change my narration
she's cement, stubborn
strongly opinionated
i'm backing down
disaster's alleviated
magenta red, gone
replaced by ocean blue
tide's retreated
nothing to pursue
look deeper, inside
mother's rainbow light
me too quick to judge
her heart's alight
experience splashed, life
knowledgeable wise
for us, her kids
she did prioritize
my mother, masterpiece
step back, admire
many facets to her
this original, I aspire

-Linda Lokhee

Ivy in the Kitchen

There's ivy hanging in the kitchen with its leaves reaching, sprouting, growing. The natural light unmasks its various shades, and the once bare window now looks like green bliss. I feel happy to have placed such beauty among beauty, such life among life.

I'm sitting in the living room - white walls, dad's chair to my right. The volume on the television is turned up a bit too high, and something political is filling the air. Another newscaster with another story has my dad tuned in. I suppose we all need a thing to believe in, something to be passionate about. I let myself smile as my dad's whole mind and body absorbs the information emanating from the screen. He's inspiring, really, the way he feels the pain of the world so easily, so attentively, with such a need to make a change.

My toes can feel winter approaching, I glance on the floor for my slippers, but I don't see them. They're probably hiding under the couch along with the rest of my forgotten things. I think to myself how I should start caring for the clutter, and myself, and maybe politics. The thoughts carry on and on. All the while, my dad thinks I'm watching the news with him, as he's unaware of my inner world.

I catch a glimpse of the ivy in the kitchen. There's suddenly a heaviness in my chest begging for attention, begging for release. The ivy reminds me of an old air plant my mom used to have when I was a young girl. We lived in many places, over few years, but the plant always came with us. Appearing as if it spread from the ceiling to the floor, it grew and grew over our worn-in, oak kitchen table. I use to admire the way it demanded its own space, allowing itself to extend into existence without hesitation, or resistance. It's green-yellow centers and white edges looked like something tangible, like something memories are made of.

How I loved that plant, and you could tell my mom loved it, too. I don't remember a single day in which the plant looked thirsty or begging for love. I don't remember a single day in which it went without water. I suppose we all need a thing to believe in, my mind whispers.

I stay seated in the leather chair, and let my thoughts wander back to these places with ease. I don't resist, I just follow them to where they need to go in this moment. My heart loosens a bit as my mind focuses on my mom. My eyes stay focused on the ivy.
I wish she loved herself in the way she loved her plant, and her children, and her husband, too. I wish she didn't let herself run dry for all those years, leaving her with almost nothing left to water.

An image of her smile spreads across my memory, leaving me in a state of ease, but suddenly her smile stiffens, and tears begin to run down her cheeks. Perhaps I have failed to see my mother's pain up until now. Perhaps my own pain has made it difficult to do so. My mom likely cried in the dark hours, wishing she could be more than life permitted for her, for us. Today, her slumped shoulders tell this story, and my body can suddenly feel the weight she once carried. I wish I could have helped her with the heaviness. I wish I could have realized the extent of her suffering before this moment.

My mind carries me through a maze of memories. I take comfort in her smile once more, and her unwavering ability to keep any hardships a secret from her children, if only for a short while. Through any sadness she endured, her arms never failed to extend softly in the night, hugging us gently when we needed the embrace. And I suppose she needed those gentle hugs, too. We were always fed, and bathed, and tickled until laughter borrowed our breath. But most notably, the plant was always lush. The plant was always vibrant, growing toward sunlight.

My mind returns to the present, and I notice my toes feel cooler than a few minutes before. The heaviness in my chest has moved to the corner of my eyelids and my lips, though heavy doesn't seem like the right word any longer. I pull the ivy from the window, begin trimming its leaves. With each piece I tend to, my heart opens and releases a bit more. A glass of water pours from my hand to the plant, each drop being soaked up like life depends on it. The soil thanks me, and the leaves do, too.

My feet lead me back to the leather seat where I wrap a purple blanket around myself. My mother's face appears before me once more, as if she had just tucked me in herself. I smile, relishing in all of the warmth she provided us with what she could. I wish I could go back and hold her hand, tell her everything would turn out just fine. I would whisper to her softly in the night and tell her her babies would be okay, and so would she. But instead I pick up the phone and dial her number. She answers, and there's a gentleness to her voice tonight. She sounds happy. We exchange conversation about work, and poetry, and even politics, too. And just before we hang up, I tell her there's ivy hanging in the kitchen reminding me of her. Reminding me of all she has allowed me to become, because of all she has ever been.

-Danielle Langin

Airbag Mother

I know it would have been easier for you to have walked away.
Instead you endured the agony of being trivialized every single day;
your spirit beaten to the ground, pride shredded to mute your sound.
And I can't for the life of me fathom how you miraculously survived
the tear-jerking roller coaster he had you conveniently ride.
An airbag, you absorbed the head on collision alone,
never letting the wreckage scathe the sanctity of our home.
Ma, you taught me everything there is to know about love;
And how chaos is a God bestowed opportunity to rise above.

-Ambica Gossain

Despite

Despite a parental divide,
we never had to run and hide.
Despite this fucked up sphere
full of judgement and fear
and even when s h o u t i n g just down the hall
was all we could h e a r,
love never wavered
with you near.
Despite the day dad died, mother,
and the heavy days that followed,
one after another,

there's **never been a doubt**
from me and my brother.

nor will there ever be a doubt, mother,
that **you've given us your all**;
that **you answered the motherly call**.

-Kevin Vargo

Silence

No clue, nor interest
In what she did or thought or felt
All day
Or before we came
What unrequited fancies she guarded
Clinging to who she used to be

Who she missed being
We cared
Only for us
For the fresh sheets on Sunday night
A chocolate cake on our special day
Someone to clap for us
Someone to hold us
We cared
Not what she stopped
Or didn't start
When we came
We cared
Not for her happiness
Or who she was or wanted to be
Her dreams and hopes
Crushed, delayed, abandoned
Angrily
Or agreeably
Who knows?
Only now
Holding my own child
Do I understand
Her silence
Her refusal to burden and ruin and mar
Such perfection
And innocence

-Lesley Worthington

Gratitudes

Giving Her The Sun

Her apricot colored shirt reminded me of the sweet tang of the fruit; it's juices always swirled down my throat like her homemade garlic remedy for my many sick days. Her choppy midnight hair never fails to give me comfort exactly like darkness does when I'm asleep. Her jade tinted raven eyes see right through my lies every single time.

I'm so (un)happy. I'm (dis)honest with her.

The best part of it all is that she's dwindling down like a flame with her internal exhaustion pipes rusting and small oil spills arising.

My mother's apricot colored shirt is now hidden in the back of the closet since she thinks it doesn't fit her anymore, she spent too much time cooking after me instead of exercising. My mother's choppy midnight hair is now beginning to fade into a soft snow, her features also falling on her face just like her knees do to the ground when she's cleaning. My mother's jade tints are now dimmed and her raven eyes don't see as sharp, working so hard every day has made them get worn out.

She was thirty seven when she had me, unknowing of harsh motherhood and the prospect of an ungrateful child.

Now I am sixteen. Now I must plant my seeds in the world after I've sucked the life out of her mighty branches and used-to-be bright emerald leaves. Well, now I can see clearly, though my glasses always seem to be blurry.

As I grow, she becomes more frail. I'm the canopy tree and she's a smaller tree closer to the ground. There's just not enough sunlight: Happiness.

I have to change. I have to clean and cook so she can feel healthy. I have to stop being lazy and make her proud so her eyes can shine. I have to ask her everyday if she's okay, if she needs help.

I'll be happy with her. I'll be honest to her.

I'll stop stealing the sun away from her.

I'll water her plants, I'll give them their light, I'll let her grow.

- Lara Decastecker

Like Mother, Like Daughter

You didn't make it easy to be your daughter and I know I didn't make it easy on you to be my mother, but we made it work with love. I know you did the best that you could, always offering more of your self than you had in you. And perhaps, that's where I learned to do the same thing too.

- Elizabeth Bonaiuto

My Mom, Her Thoughts

A spring evening in winter it was,
Me and mom en route shopping;
New bags I needed to buy soon,
The choices of color, open to mom.

First bend in twilight, then right,
Known shops to our left we walked,
Lighting the usual streets in dark;
Not many pedestrians to accompany.

Greeted we were of a sudden!
An elderly shopkeeper known to us,
Life seemed pitiless on him,
Complaining about children he came.

Luck betrayed him, he said.
His days seemed lost in darkness,
One daughter, in a failed marriage.
One son, living far away.

But his daughter retained her job,
Up on her feet, divorce not her fault!
A cookie of income, the son sent back.
Well being of father he cared about.

Why still unhappy? My mother asked.
Why not contended with little of life?
Sparkles small reminding us to live,
Mom explained to him her belief.

Share market investment, my son is not!
He is the love I promised to raise.
And I would continue to do so,
Until the end of time, end of days.

This I do, without hopes of return!
He will come to aid if raised well.
I believe in him, honest and fair;
He will be a good man, in good faith.

Taken aback by this thought I was.
In my heart, I still knew not things;
Things, my mom would not share.
Either with me, or anyone near.

The shopkeeper smiled, and smiled again.
You are right my child, he said.
Patting my back the old man sighed,
A very lucky mom you have my boy!

We had to take our leave then.
Pacing, we moved along our way.
But I will not forget the two smiles,
The smiles, my mom painted that day!

-Debjeet Mukherjee

A Candid Grace

Hold tight her fondness of things
Her losses are her strength
And that is where you find her kindness
Hold dear her worry for you
Your safety is her life
And that is where you find her love
Let in her cautionary tales
Her insight holds the merit
And that is where you find her wisdom
Reflect her love back to her
Contemplate her grace
Amongst her torment
Laying to rest her husband
And first born son, your brother
Be silent in wonder
Her life, your mother

-Gregory Oman

02.04.19

Dear Mom —
I forgive you.
For everything
I just hope
That one day I can forgive myself
I'm working on it — day by day
And I'll keep working on it every day
I just hope that you know
I have and always will love you

-LiAnnah Jameson

Looking Back

Gratitudes

A Mother's Love

A mother will hold her babies
in her arms as long as possible.
Then she will continue to hold them
in her heart
forever.

- Angela Marie Niemiec

Home From Work

in.
turn.
pop goes the lock.

down the hall
of our ranch-style home
with my dreamy mind,
toy story legos,
hot wheels cars,
and my imagination
a millions miles wide,

i could hear.

i could hear that sound.
that sound from anywhere,
that sound so settling,
that sound, anytime,

Looking Back

that sound
so indicative.

and in through the door
after a long day of work,
you finally made your way.

i can remember it always:

'hi mommy, i missed you!
i can't wait to tell you about my day!'

but oh, only now, only now
am i able to understand
what a brilliant mother it made you.

for after days, weeks, months, and years
of work and stress,
you'd come home with a smile on your face
and love in your heart.
all
while still finding the time to play.

-Kevin Vargo

The Nest

we jump from the nest early,
wings underdeveloped,

& she prays fervently
with eyes closed
& then open just long
enough to spot us still
moving across
an endless sky
& then closed again.

she wonders:
what calls us so early
from
our small & safe worlds?

& what can she do but
watch in horror?
in hope?

-Emily Adams-Aucoin

Angelic Purity

Biblical teachings
Spoke ill of the divorced
How could you take on
Such burdens that were not yours?

Stepping up
Stepping in
Step Mom and friend.

Showering with love
Judgment be damned,
You took our hearts
As you led us by hand.

Never could we have asked
For a Mom such as you
Giving us beauty
As only your pure heart could do.

You worked magic in the home
You worked magic in our lives
You wove us a world
Removed from the outside.

You picked us
When you could have walked away,
You chose to be our mother
Even when it was hard to stay,
Even when we were bad
Never did we feel you regretted the choice
To marry our Dad.

-Austie M. Baird

Gratitudes

Courage

Arthritic fingers are caressed
by the gentle hand
of my mother.
Perched on a hard seat,
by a cold bed,
surrounded by white walls,
unforgiving.
A picture,
straight out of a textbook,
an end of life pamphlet.
Strength is hidden
behind tired eyes.
A caregiver by nature,
an angel, not of the heavens,
but of Earth.
The same blood that flows
through the veins of my mother,
and her mother before her,
courses through my own.
The profile, I have
inherited:
High cheekbones,
a dainty chin.
But I descend from a
line of strong women.
Courage,
it seems,
is also in my DNA.

-Sara Kelly

Birds

I feel as if the only gifts
I can give to you
are sliced words.
Words I wrap in
colourful sentences

and place neatly under your chin,
I watch them melt into your skin
like the hemp cream by your bed.

But when you act for me
or speak for me
or hurt for me,
how can I kill the need
to heal you with verses?

It doesn't feel like enough
for all the times you've put
your foot between me and the spiral.
I want to sweeten air for you
and teach the thunder your favourite songs.
I want to summon God for you
and give your pain to the birds
to carry into the sky and drop like stones,
but no, I just have words.

It seems as if the only mirror willing
to reflect my heart is this page,
another mirror to watch me age
along with your eyes,
so like mine.

These words exist only for you
and although they will never be
laced with gold
or shine underground,
I can promise they will be underneath your pillow
when the night is long and dark.

-Maya Elphick

Steps

Three kids,
And a single dad.

Never did we see you cringe,
At the world we had.

Stepping in,
Stepping up.

Demonstrating "step" and parent
can go hand in hand,

When those steps
Are towards hearts and mind.

No walls,
No fear.

Simple love to make it all clear.

Clear we were loved.
Clear we were wanted.
Clear we were enough
For you to *want* to be bonded.

-Austie M. Baird

Thank You for the Whispers

Lullabies are whispers
Gently to new ears
Mother's soothing love songs
Calming infant fears
Calming also Mother's
Worries, cleansed by tears
Joy mixed up with wonder
Hopes and dreams so dear
Now it's time to thank you
After all these years
For whispers still remembered
That echo in old ears

-Russell E. Willis

Change the World

my father
the protector
shielding me
from the cruel and angry world
my mother
the manifester
teaching me
i could change it

-M.R.S.

Twilight

mother unfolds her gentle hands
and the twilight turns to night
the dark, *she says*
and the moon so bright
was always meant for us
dreamers and witches
lost and lonely
women with artist souls
trapped in manmade daylight
mothers birth nights like these
where billions of stars adorn the skies
and the chaos of creation
is a symphony of destruction
and somehow the dark
is so beautifully brighter alone
while daylight's unforgiving
prelude to the death of a dream
we women are night walkers
in communion with existence
we are the necessary cosmic chaos
destruction and creation dancing in tandem
our voices the prelude to resistance
we will always ring out as many
solidly grip hands held high
as one alone, together
we rise

-RJK

Symbiotic Blessings

Each year the flying ants would come
Covering the back deck
Black backs and translucent wings
Reflecting in the warmth of the spring sun.

She taught me that those ants
Cantankerous as could be
Came to bring the gift
Of setting peonies free.

Trapped closed by sticky sap
They could not fully bloom
And the annoyance of the ants
Meant beauty arriving soon.

My mother raised me in that way
To find the purpose and beauty in all
So that I can see those ants descend
And find blessing in their fall.

-Austie M. Baird

:Generations:

Reflections

She stared back at me. From my father's eyes, her mother's cheek bones. Her determined frizzy hair, an imperfect halo.

I can forget her for days. And have. In the frantic pace of motherhood, and climbing ladders, and doing what I do. But then I'm stilled. I reflect. On her. She reflects. In me. It's clear. It's all mixed up. These moments at the mirror unsettle me. Then settle me.

Imperfections once magnified, blown up, are now so small. So trite. Such hanging on to slights and hurts. To offhand comments, context long ago forgotten. These pits and scars becoming shadowed ghosts, as the view expands. They are nothing. As we rise above looking down. Looking back. Seeing the whole.

Imagine. Letting go. And rising even higher. Such beauty and perfection. Right there.

I mustn't be dragged down by petty remembrances. Poked and prodded until they fester, all weepy. Burning and aching each time I visit.

No, I must rise above.

I blink myself back to now. And see my daughter staring back. My daughter's eyes in mine. That bottom lip. I am stilled again. When she sees me in her mid-life mirror will she be tender and forgiving and see only the love and grace of mother and daughter. As I see so clearly now.

-Lesley Worthington

A Mother's Love

I look up, feeling the subtle brush of a comforting gust and I know it's you, calling to me, from just beyond where the sky meets the horizon. I blink, repeatedly, hoping you're near; and when you finally appear, you're glowing, smiling from ear to ear. Your reassuring presence transcends through the silence, as the sun illuminates my disbelieving irises. I know this isn't real, but oh how I wish you were really here! I don't bother with anything to say, allowing my tears to convey what you more than anyone knows mom: that my heart hurts, that I love you, that I need you even more now than before. I search your face, focusing directly into your gaze and what I see reflected doesn't surprise me. I recognize It's the same care and guidance I give to my son, that through me, you still continue in providing.

-Elizabeth Bonaiuto

Our Love Collides

My arms cradle him
to my chest as I hold her
hand in mine
the monitor beeps in the
darkness as the moon creeps
through the blind
All I know is in this
room beyond these walls
stars burn
bright in a sky of unknown
depths but still the world
must turn
And when my sun comes tumbling
down my heart a
shattered star
the broken fragments fall
to earth but his love
ignites the shards
I hold him close
as I watch her drift
away on the ocean tide;
becoming a mother
while losing my own
but through him
our Worlds
collide

-Abi Hayes

Apologies

for every time i told you, "no!"
for every time i cried,
for every time i slammed the door,
for every time i lied
for the drama you must have endured,
for accumulated gray hair,
for the multiple sleepless nights,
for the never ending care
for my actions -- i apologize,
for your love -- i give you praise,
for i understand the difficulty
when a child, you do raise

-Krystal Centinello

Summoning the Shechinah:
Baking Challah with my Daughter on Friday Morning

      Hands dipped white,
      words and measurements laid out
      on the counter before us

we will you into our world.
Impossibly weighted,
three-dimensional

      we will your shimmering particles into water,
      knead you condensed and pliant,
      amazed at your own resilience.

You are warm,
caressed and battered
by so many asking hands

      you grow soft,
      allow yourself
      to be lovingly braided.

Now you stretch and rise
into the thick wonder of physical form;
you harden a skin of your own.

      This Sabbath may you dwell with us,
      in us, under a white cloth roof,
      rooted, still reaching.

You are the sweetness in our mouths,
the hope that one day
we can reverse the incantation:
      take the heaviness of who we are
      and knead it back
      into light.

- Yiskah Rosenfeld

Gratitudes

If Family is a Meal, Mom is the Challah

If my mother believed in God, which she didn't, it was only so she could have someone other than basketball referees and Republicans to argue with. She fled far from her New York roots to the Bible belt, raising her three daughters in Kansas. Sure, she served as president of our Jewish community for several years, but she only went to Friday night services for the schmoozing and cake. My mother never wanted to take credit for my love of Jewish tradition. She said I was born this way. But it was my secular, swear-like-a-sailor Mom who taught me the two most important elements of Judaism: food and love.

Food, of course, has been central to the Jewish tradition long before Mom came along. All important Jewish events revolved around food, from the forbidden fruit in the Garden of Eden to the medieval tradition of feeding toddlers cakes topped with holy words scrawled in honey when it was time to wean. While two thousand years ago food - in the form of sacrifices that also fed the Priestly caste - formed the center of Jewish life at the Temple, called The Holy House in Biblical Hebrew, later these rituals moved to a smaller "house," the Jewish home, with the Sabbath dinner on Friday night mimicking the sacrificial meals eaten by the High Priests. The rabbis noticed that the word for heart, lev, has the numerology of 32, the number of teeth in the human mouth. Thus they
affirmed that the way to someone's heart really is through their stomach.

For my mother, food was never a substitute for love, but a conduit. It is both a pathway to childhood memory, with her google maps sending her through a route of liver, bananas, licorice, and her grandmother's

slippery chicken soup (though not always together!), and the centerpiece of family and friendship. Her Holy of Holies has always
been the dining room table, an altar that draws her loved ones together. Often the last to sit down at a meal as she dashed to and fro from the kitchen, she was incapable of leaving the table once there, refusing to acknowledge when the time came for her family and friends to scatter.

    We were not a family that celebrated Shabbat, the Jewish Sabbath, every Friday night. Mostly that happened for a few weeks after we kids returned from Jewish summer camp, believing we'd faithfully keep the Sabbath laws forever, and not just until school started. But after my father inherited his mother's candlesticks, my mother's enthusiasm was ignited, and we gathered at the table with the two candles, a silver cup of sweet red wine, and a loaf of braided bread covered with a white cloth. The two candles are said to represent the extra bit of soul we receive when the Shechina, the feminine aspect of the divine - sometimes seen as bride or wife and mother, other times as daughter - comes to dwell each Friday night, riding on the wings of the sunset. In Kansas, our Friday night dinners weren't quite that romantic, with the usual sibling squabbles and my older sisters
begging to be excused to go out with their friends. But everyone came together, and that's
what my mother wanted most.

    Challah beautifully represents Mom's nurturing qualities. A sweet bread that must be made with love and patience, it is the central food of Jewish ritual and memory. Rabbinic legend teaches that the tradition of lighting the Sabbath candles and blessing the bread and wine was first passed from the Biblical character of Sarah to her daughter-in-law Rebecca. The braids might represent the passing of tradition through three generations, from my Grandma Miriam, who was the first

female pharmacist in Oregon after graduating college at 16, to my mother, a housewife-turned-financial whiz and the daughter of a first generation American refridgerator repairman in New York, to her children, keeping the tiny Jewish community alive in Kansas. (When my friends say,
You're from Kansas? I didn't know there were Jewish people in Kansas! I reply drolly, Not anymore. . .) Or they might represent the weaving together of the family and friends both near and far.

    The word Challah refers not only to the bread itself, but to a piece of the dough that is removed before baking. Originally this was an act of tithing to set aside a portion for the High Priest; now it is a symbol that reminds us of tzedakah, charity, of saving something to give back to the community. This passion for tzedakah, entwined in Judaism with tzedek, justice, has always been my Mom's greatest gift. She was the champion of the underdog, and one of the first to offer food and love when a friend or family member was sick. And she didn't just cook up the traditional chicken soup, oh no. She'd carefully consider what she thought that person's favorite food was, or what they'd eaten together at some point. One time she attempted Italian meatballs, another time she tried adding beets. She had an enormous heart, and cared deeply about community. Though my mom never taught me how to make challah, she has taught me again and again how to set aside a portion for others.

    I never married. But at the age of 44, I conceived a child of my own. And sure enough, my kid was born a religious fanatic, obsessed with celebrating Shabbat, even when I just wanted to go out for burritos or settle in with a movie on Netflix. I sent her to a Jewish preschool, where they made challah every week and learned the blessings and songs. Since then we have experimented, more and less successfully, with making challah at home. We light candles and I imagine us in that long chain of tradition from Sarah in her tent in Mesopotamia to our modest rental in Berkeley. Born in a boy's body, my child is transgender, adopting female pronouns over two years ago in 1st grade. My mother, with her generous heart, never blinked an eye at the change, and has always loved my daughter unconditionally. And so my daughter and I fill the cup with juice, cover the challah (so it won't be embarrassed that the wine is blessed first), and light the candles, first drawing the light toward us through circling our hands, then closing our eyes. She sings the blessings with an out of tune ukulele before tearing off an enormous piece of the stretchy, warm bread, sometimes covered in cinnamon or sprinkles, sometimes braided creatively in 6 or 7 parts. We put quarters in a tzedakah box for charity and say prayers of healing for my mother, now in a memory care home in Kansas. Though she always knows who we are, and on our last enjoyed celebrating Hannukah with us and showing off her grandchild, in the last few weeks she has begun to lose her ability to speak and swallow.

Thank you, Mom, for teaching me to love unconditionally and give generously. Here are
some other things you taught me. I will do my best to pass these family traditions down
to your beautiful granddaughter:

- Any sickness can be healed with an egg and toast.
- Always buy too much Halloween candy, and make sure it's your favorite kind.
- The words we say on Passover, "Let all who are hungry come and eat" is just a
- Jewish mother's way of saying, "Oy, I made too much food again this year."
- Food and love. For better or for worse, you should always have a little too much of both.

- Yiskah Rosenfeld

Gratitudes

Memories & Wishes

You Will Know

I have so much more to say to you
Questions I want to ask
One of the hardest times for us all
Is when you took your last breath
I felt a bit like a child again
The night that we lost you
I know now when I need your words
You are just a thought away
Your wisdom, it come back to me
I hear it, just as you spoke it
'Listen to your heart', you'd say
And 'never ignore your gut
Keep your head, you'll need to think
But do not let that rule you'
If I asked you something difficult
You couldn't possibly answer
I always said 'how will I know'
And this, your only answer
'When the time is right to know
I promise you, you'll know it'
I've grown to understand your words
They come right when I need them
Your love is all around me still
I know because I feel it
Sometimes it seems we're far away
These times I tune into my heart
It does me good to hear you there
And reminds me we're never apart

-Andigrace

Gratitudes

The Little Things

What I miss the most are the things I used to take for granted. The mouth watering aromas coming out of your kitchen, your way of filling our bellies with love. Feeling embarrassed when you would sing or start dancing wherever we were. Your need to control everything, to ensure that we were taken care of. The colorful Spanish language you left on my voice mail, when I was too selfish to pick up the phone. Oh what I would give to hear your voice or for one more of your hugs.

- Elizabeth Bonaiuto

Sentinel

A stack of cards
My loved ones gone
Not one by one
But all of a sudden
As if they asked
If I remembered
But rest assured
I've never forgotten
I will guard all of these
Pure, unfiltered memories

-Greg Oman

Bare Snow

Mother,
how you wore forever
    like the leaves that remain
    like the leaves that bare snow.
I used to wonder if you were cold,
    but all you'd ever say was
    "How lovely"
while pointing at
the angels we made in the snow
that
    somehow
        always
            looked like you.

- L. T. Pelle

Sunset

When darkness falls,
I'm going to be there
in the short seconds.
I'll hold the minutes open
to let you squeeze through
and save the memories
from the metronome.

When your eyes forget to know me
and the night is on your shoulder,
don't doubt tomorrow's sunrise,
as it will come.

-Maya Elphick

Mommy Dearest

I've celebrated my 29th birthday
More than once already
Yet all I want right now
All I yearn for
Is my mother

Yes — Here I am
A woman in her 30's
No longer a child
But wishing that I were

But now I find myself in the role
Of the caregiver to my mother
And right now — I am the one who needs
her
More than anyone else in my life

Dementia has turned her into
A childlike version of herself
And I feel as if I am the parent
When right now a parent is what I need

Nobody can fill the gap — an open, bleeding wound
That only my mother could cauterize
With everything going on in my life

No matter our differences from the past
I know that I could break down to her
Cry, complain, and overreact like my life is ending
Over the smallest little thing — or a big thing
And she wouldn't judge me or tell me to just

"Get over it"
Or

"Move on"

As so many other people have told me so far
She would listen to every word and wipe away every
tear
She would understand
And that's the best anyone
Can ask for in this world

I miss you, Mom

-LiAnnah Jameson

You See

You wouldn't have wanted
the boy chasing the wind
to trip over his shoelaces,

You wouldn't have wanted that girl
to say *'i'* instead of *'y'* in gypsy
at the spelling bee,

You wouldn't have wanted
that tetherball to swoop around and
pound my face dizzy and red,

You wouldn't have wanted lava tag to end.

No, you wouldn't have wanted that at all.

You did want that stray Rottweiler
at Tulalip Shores, you'd call him *Brindle*,
growling and drooling pools all day
as his eyes watched the waves
as his paws sunk in sand.

You'd bake him birthday cake
and he'd smile—twice a year—
to make up for all the missed ones.

A worn hat
covered the chemo.
I never noticed.

We played putt-putt at Kayak Point
every Saturday.
You liked the colored balls,
pinks and purples.
I rolled the white ones.

I went back there.
Walked the course.
The greens were grown over
long enough to bend in the wind
the balls in the ponds were scummy—
even the pinks and purples.

I rubbed the weary wooden posts,
one read
par 3 feet: 73
and the final one—
do you remember that one?
A full 100 feet.

What is salt if not the ocean's precursor?
What is love if not grief's?

Your eyes ceased mourning,
but your eyes are in mine,
and mine do, mine do.

Mary Carol Gardner, 1928-2001

-Tor Strand

Dance

I watch her hands,
how they weave & mend,
weave & mend.
a dance to bring in
the new day.

-Emily Adams-Aucoin

My Mother Divine

There she sits, frailty slightly brushing by
Gracefully ageing, woman beautified
Each wrinkle etched tells a story of times
a fulfilling life lived, within those lines
Once confidence bloomed, now less self assured
due to hardships, circumstances endured
Now I'm older, I look at her and see
a mix of Oak and Cherry Blossom tree
My heritage of strength, love and beauty
devotion not from filial duty
Admiration, gratitude for she's mine
Approbation to my Mother divine

-Linda Lokhee

A: De:

Mother dear
My angel
I know you see me now
I know you know
Just what I've done
I hope I make you proud
I can find you
In the rainbows
I hear you
In the clouds
I feel your touch
Against my skin
When the pain I hold
Gets loud
I hope you know
I love you
Although I've never said
In sound
But every part
Of who I am
Just longs to see
Your smile
I could have done

It better
I've just had my share
Of trials
I've fought hard to keep
This sense of me
Through all these
Weathered miles
But it's the love
I kept from you
That helped me
Through denial
It's the safe
You gave
The dreams I've saved
From when I was a child
You always are inside
I can feel you all around
My mom, my pride
My guide through life
I miss you
Love;
Your girl

-Megan Hann

What I Want (Choose) to Remember

Making snow ice cream every winter
And jumping in puddles after a hard rain
Where the water had collected
In the potholes on the side streets
Sharing two cups of hot tea with milk and sugar
(You always liked more milk than sugar
    I always liked more sugar than milk)

How you made the best chicken tenders I've ever tasted
(Now I'll never learn how to make them like you)
On weekends, we would make popcorn
And you would melt vanilla icing in the microwave
We would take the salty popcorn and dip it in the icing
I haven't done that in so many years
(I'm going to buy popcorn this weekend
    And vanilla icing to share with my nephews)

Mornings before school when you'd wake me up
And let me toss a blanket over the heater in the floor
With a plastic protector which made the blanket
Rise like hot, homemade rolls in the oven
The warm heat would lull me back to sleep
While you made me my "special" breakfast:
Oatmeal with smiley faces made out of jelly

At night, you'd heat up pans on the stove
And right before you tucked me in
You'd run the hot pan under the sheets
So that I always climbed into a warm, toasty bed
Then you would sing me a song
"Ballad of Louise" by Jeannie C. Riley
(Probably not what most moms would sing
    to their pre-teen daughters)

But I always loved the way the words
Spilled softly from your lips
(I still don't know the second verse by heart
      But I'm working on it)

You'd tell me that if I had trouble sleeping
To close my eyes and imagine a stark white room
Four walls, a ceiling, and floor — all white
And slowly paint that room black
Imagining each stroke of the paintbrush
(I was always asleep before the whole room was painted)

These are the things I want to remember about you
I don't want to remember when you got sick
And couldn't take care of yourself
I don't want to remember having to feed you meals
Or watching you struggle for twenty minutes
Just to get in or out of a car, watching your crystal
      blue eyes
Well up with tears of frustration and confusion
I don't want to remember the smell of piss and
      ammonia
The beeping of machines that keep people alive
As I walk down the long hallway to your room at the
      nursing home
I don't want to remember you as the woman who has
      become a stranger
You know me, but I don't recognize you
At least - not the you that I want to recognize and
      remember
I want to remember you from long ago
Before you and dad got a divorce
When you put over fifty glow-in-the-dark stars
On the ceiling over my bed
And you'd sing me a lullaby
That you wrote yourself

About us sitting by a river
Underneath the shade of a tree

(I wish I could remember
    More than the first few lines...
        ...One day I'll finish it for us)

- LiAnnah Jameson

Holy

I am still reaching
for the meaning of holy.
I heard it was something beautiful,
I felt it in your hands
as they held me
and wished for a life of kindness.

-Maya Elphick

Grateful

Thank you, for all the time I could spend with you
Thank you, for all the hardships you helped me through
Thank you, for being my best friend
To share my tears and laughter
Thank you, for believing in me
You showed me who I want to be
Thank you, for making me the woman I am today
I wish that you could stay, just a little longer
So much I want to share with you,
so much I wish that you could see
So many beautiful memories,
I'll carry them forever with me

-Lizzy in Words

Driving My Mother to Acupuncture in Kansas

Reiko sets me
in the one chair at the back
of the house with the red door
on the street my mother
always forgets to turn onto.
Shoes line the entrance.

Books line the walls.
Japanese and English trickle their spines
while down the hall my mother
removes her wig, hair thinned
to reddish cobwebs, the scalp almost sexual
in its sudden exposure.

In the one chair in the empty room
I read the Bible, run my tongue
down the blessings and curses
and taste the old rules of childhood:
curses are caused; blessings are luck,
chance baskets arriving by wind.

Inside my mother the gift, unbidden, flowers.
Who sent it? The day warm and breezy
as if earned by good behavior,
but inside her breast, the curse,
condensed to a not-ripe fruit,
a second, smaller heart.

Reiko boils water for tea,
serves me medallions of candied ginger,
sweet rolled leaves of seaweed.
I don't know what I've done
to deserve this, the cup smaller than my hand,
tea hot and swollen with peach.

Sweetness pins the galaxy's center
to this chair, at this moment;
my mother's muted voice softly orbits.
Sugar and sour, blessing and curse,
my mouth accepts how they coexist,
how an empty room makes room in any language.

I think of the shoes
lined up at the door like obedient horses,
how whatever is stowed in our hearts,
mother, daughter, bitter, sweet,
the shoes will bear us up, the shoes will take us
where we need to go.

-Yiskah Rosenfeld

Transcending love

how do you put to words your source of life
your source of light and love
time flashing before my eyes
a lifetime running by of you and I

should I call it the greatest love story of all times
a mother and her child
a bond that can cross time and space
for nothing could contain the love inside your heart
and words could not describe it or set it apart

you were the centre of my existence
the air that I would breathe
until the universe shook at its core
and you flew away from me, to your eternal home
and yet still there you are in everything I do, in everything I see
like a love song haunting me

brown eyes radiating pure soul light
how can you not be the brightest star in my darkest nights
your love could move many mountains
maybe even stop the pouring rain

nothing I could say would ever do you justice
words would be in vain
so sometimes words come out as tears
to find a way to speak that which my mouth can't say

oh, I know we weren't perfect
very far from at times
but now that you are gone
I got to know you even better
and I see were we went wrong

but there is no room for what ifs and maybes
they wouldn't do me any good
I can only be grateful to have known a love so true

for there by my side you stood
carrying me when I couldn't carry myself
and I did the same for you
we both did what we could

where you would go I would follow
and yes it saddens me
that now I'm standing on my own
although I am not all alone
it will never be the same

my heart still beats so I carry on
trying to make you proud
we'll meet in my dreams
where our love stays alive
creating new memories still

and when the time comes I hope to be blessed
for the image I wish to behold
- of the magnificent wings you must carry
if they reflect your soul -
then I'll unfold mine and take the leap
to meet you at Home

but only when the time has come

- Lizzy in Words

Gratitudes

In Memory of Marit Josten Highland

I.
She lived for a century.
Through the fickle decades of America,
fun and woe ebbing and flowing
like the pink sea shells
on her Camano Island
beach home.
She would ask me to go find them,
those blushing shells
no larger or redder than a pinky nail
and I would. And she would say,
"Well, how 'bout that."
And she would say,
"Those shells used to fill the sand.
Not anymore."

II.
She was a snappy woman.
Not in an ill way,
rather like the gingersnaps
that always filled the glass jar
on her countertop.
She would send me with lengthy directions—
to the left, to the right, down steep-set stairs
to the right, to the left—
"There you'll find the icebox with the soda-pop."
In later years she rocked
in a living room chair.
A telephone with extra-large numbers
on her left, a window on her right,
where the Sound rippled
with orcas deep beneath.
Her eyes tired, days dimmed,

but her mind went on,
aware of every drawer,
shelf, and box under her roof.
"The bright days used to be grey,
now even the Sound's gone."
She ate meals with slow gratitude.
"Kinda tasty," she'd say,
and when it was time to part,
"Now you kids behave yourself,"
to my parents. And,
"You be a good boy now,"
in my own ear.

III.

Once I asked her where college was.
She laughed, "Work was college."
Eyebrows raised, "Anywhere you could find it."
They placed her in the kitchen
when the world was at war.
She was never one for the apron,
so she became a typist.
"I was a whiz on those keys."
The 4th of July parade
runs in front of her hand-bricked home
on Utsalady road.
When I was a boy,
she'd ask me to guide her down the front steps,
hand in hand—
"I need to keep an eye on all the commotion."

-Tor Strand

Competition Winners

Gratitudes: To Our Mothers, was born in a large part out of a writing competition held by A.B.Baird Publishing — these are the winners of that competition.

Grand Prize:
"A Mother Without Patience" Emily Louise Witthohn

First Runner Up:
"My Mother Divine" Linda Lokhee

Second Runners Up:
"She Taught Me This" Angela Marie Neimiec
"Collecting Calls" Dre Jones

People's Choice:
"God" Ambica Gossain

Index

A listing of each author found in this anthology and which pages you can find their work.

Abi Hayes: 65
Ambica Gossain: 20, 25, 43
Andigrace: 73
Andrew C. Ulon: 13
Angela Marie Niemiec: 7, 52
Araz Sharma: 29
Austie M. Baird: 4, 6, 9, 13, 55, 58, 61
Ben Hand: 24
Danielle Langin: 40
Debjeet Mukherjee: 48
Dre Jones: 10, 21
Elizabeth Bonaiuto: 48, 64, 74
Emily Adams- Aucoin: 8, 11, 12, 54, 80
Emily Louise Witthohn: 35
Erica Rolston: 18
Gregory Oman: 50
Kevin Vargo: 11, 23, 44, 52
Krystal Centinello: 66
L.T. Pelle: 20, 22, 75
Lacie Wright: 19
Lara Decastecker: 17, 47
Lesley Worthington: 50, 77, 85
LiAnnah Jameson: 50, 77, 82
Linda Lokhee: 39, 80
Lizzy in Words: 85, 88
M.R.S: 5, 6, 8, 34, 59
Mari Antoinette: 24
Maya Ephick: 19, 20, 33, 57, 75, 84
Megan Fulton: 16

Gratitudes

Megan Hann: 81
RJK: 60
Russell E. Willis: 59
Sara Kelly: 5, 26
Sophia Luna: 38
Tor Strand: 79, 90
Yiskah Rosenfeld: 67, 68, 86

Gratitudes

Dear Readers,

As always, we at A.B.Baird Publishing believe that all our writers are incredibly talented and encourage you to explore new writers often! You can find the Instagram handles for the writers listed at the front of the book.

Our goals here at A.B.Baird Publishing center on continuing to empower writers by giving social media based authors as many avenues as possible towards publication. If you are interested in how you can become published, or want to stay up to date on our latest ventures, please join our email list on our website **www.abbairdpublishing.com** or visit us on instagram @a.b.baird_publishing.

Your reviews mean more to us than you realize! One of the keys to continued success is having reviews on sites such as Amazon. If you have enjoyed this anthology we as that you please let us know by leaving reviews on the amazon listing. In addition we always encourage you to check out the authors on their social media accounts and let them know what you think of their work!

Thank you for your support- without you, we would be nothing!

Austie Baird — Owner
A.B.Baird Publishing

Gratitudes

In Loving Memory of:
Julie Rae Gregory

Nov. 26th, 1969 - March 31st, 2019

Loving Wife, Mother, Nanny, Daughter, Sister and Friend...

May we all strive to be a little more like you, each and every day.

www.ingramcontent.com/pod-product-compliance
Lightning Source LLC
Chambersburg PA
CBHW031453040426
42444CB00007B/1089